KEN ROBBINS

FOOD FOR THOUGHT

THE STORIES BEHIND THE THINGS WE EAT

A NEAL PORTER BOOK

ROARING BROOK PRESS

NEW YORK

ACKNOWLEDGMENTS

The author wishes to thank the following: Tony Heidrich, and at the Australian Banana Growers Council,
Jane Milburn, media consultant to the same; Martha Corrozi of the Water Resources Agency—part of the
Institute for Public Administration at the University of Delaware—for the photo of the mushroom-growing
room on page 45; Michael Wood for the *Amanita muscaria* photo on page 44—his Web site,
www.mykoweb.com, is a fabulous resource for anyone interested in mycology;
Martin Gardener of California Gardens for the pomegranate tree photo on page 37.

Designed by Impress, Inc., www.impressinc.com
Distributed in Canada by H. B. Fenn and Company Ltd.

Library of Congress Cataloging-in-Publication Data
Robbins, Ken.
Food for thought / Ken Robbins.—1st. ed.
p. cm.
"A Neal Porter book."
ISBN-13: 978-1-59643-343-4
ISBN-10: 1-59643-343-4
1. Food. 2. Food—Folklore. 1. Title
TX355.R54 2008
641.3—dc22
2007044062

Roaring Brook Press books are available for special promotions and premiums.
For details contact: Director of Special Markets, Holtzbrinck Publishers.

First edition March 2009
Printed in China

1 3 5 7 9 10 8 6 4 2

For Tatiana

INTRODUCTION

APPLES, ORANGES, POTATOES, tomatoes, grapes, bananas, mushrooms, corn, and pomegranates—they come from all the corners of the earth. Some are staples of our diets; some are treats. But what they have in common is that they are available in every supermarket in America. Each of them has played an important part in our history, not only affecting what we choose to eat, but, in some cases, who survives and who starves, who has work and who does not. These foods appear in great art as well as cartoons, in folktales as well as literature, and in jokes as well as ancient myths.

Every kind of food has its story. Here are just a few of them.

APPLES

FOR MILLIONS OF YEARS, we humans, as well as other less-developed species, hunted for meat and scrounged for whatever edible fruits and berries and other growing things we could find. Eventually, perhaps 12,000 years ago, we learned to grow our own food—and when we did, apples were probably the very first fruits we grew. So apples are quite old, and even the name is old: it comes from an ancient Indo-European word, *abl*. In Latin, the language of the ancient Romans, the word for apple was *malus*. There is a city in Kazakhstan called Alma-Ata, which means "Father of Apples." Nobody knows for sure, but it's likely that the wild ancestors of apples we eat today were first grown in that part of the world.

Now apples are grown nearly everywhere the temperature is moderate. People say "as American as apple pie," yet for a fruit so closely associated with America, it's a little surprising to learn that China grows almost half the apples in the world today, nearly seven times more than the United States.

Apples appear in many ancient myths and stories. In one, the Norse goddess Idunn was the keeper of some rather special apples. It seems that the other Norse gods needed to eat them in order to stay young and immortal. But one day, Idunn was kidnapped, and the Aesir (that's what the Norse gods were called) started to get gray and wrinkled and a little thick in the middle. They had to send the god Loki to rescue her so they could have their apples again and stay young.

IN GREEK MYTHOLOGY, Atalanta was a great hunter, and she could run faster than any man. Her father, who wanted her to get married, made her a bet she thought she couldn't lose: if a suitor beat her in a race, she would marry him; if he lost, he would die. For a while, it worked out fine for Atalanta, though not so well for her suitors. But, eventually, a man named Hippomenes entered the race. He had gotten hold of three golden apples, which he threw down at crucial moments in the race to distract Atalanta. (Not really fair, but there you have it.) Each time she stopped to pick up an apple, of course, it slowed her down. Hippomenes won the race and Atalanta, too.

Hercules, another character from ancient Greek mythology, was the original superhero. A huge, strong lout, he hardly knew his own strength, and he went crazy, killing his own wife and child. To make up for this horrible crime, he was given 12 tasks, or labors. One of them was to steal some golden apples from the garden of the Hesperides (not the ones Hippomenes used to trick Atalanta—other ones).

ANOTHER FAMOUS MYTH involving apples is about the start of a war. There was once a very fancy wedding between Peleus, a mortal, and Thetis, a goddess. All kinds of important people were there, and all the gods, too, except Eris, the goddess of strife, who hadn't been invited. To make trouble, she rolled a golden apple onto the floor among the wedding guests. (Not one of the apples used by Hippomenes or stolen

by Hercules—yet another one.) On the apple was written: FOR THE MOST BEAUTIFUL. Hera, the queen of the gods; Aphrodite, the goddess of love; and Athena, the goddess of wisdom, each thought it beyond question that she deserved the apple, so it was decided that Paris, the mortal prince of Troy, would choose the goddess most deserving the apple. To bribe him, Aphrodite promised him the love of the most beautiful woman in the world, Helen of Sparta. The trouble was, Helen was already married to Menelaus, a powerful king. When Helen ran off with Paris, the result was the terrible Trojan War, which Homer described in a great epic poem, the *Iliad*. The fighting cost many lives and caused the downfall of Troy. All because of an apple.

OF COURSE, the most famous apple story is the one about the biblical characters Adam and Eve, the first two people in the world. They were created by God, who meant for them to live—naked, innocent, and happy forever—in a paradise called Eden. Though they could have anything else they wanted, God told them very plainly and very sternly never, ever to eat the fruit of the tree of knowledge. Well, there was an evil, twisted snake in that garden, and that snake whispered to Eve, and Eve whispered to Adam, and before you knew it, they had eaten that fruit, and before they knew it, they were thrown straight out of paradise. They did slowly begin getting on with their lives, begetting children who begat more children who eventually peopled the entire world. But things were really never the same.

Now, no one knows if the tree of knowledge was really an apple tree. The Bible, from which this story comes, never actually says so. Apples weren't known to grow back then in the Middle East, where this story is said to take place. But it's one of those things that many people just figure they know, because that's how the story has always been told: it was an apple, sweet and juicy and forbidden, that caused all the trouble.

There's the legend of Isaac Newton and the apple. (Anything called a legend generally makes a nice story, but it is almost never true.) It's said that Newton was sitting under an apple tree when a falling apple bonked him on the head and prompted him to invent his theory of gravity. It's a nice story.

FINALLY, in more recent times, there is another nice story, this one about John Chapman, also called Johnny Appleseed. In the 1800s, he was so impressed with the healthy benefits and wonderful taste of apples that he traveled by foot, clearing land in the wilderness and planting apple trees across large parts of Ohio, Indiana, and Illinois. It's said that some of the orchards he planted still exist today.

Apple computers were named for the fruit. The bulge in front of your neck (it's bigger in men than in women, but we all have one) is called an Adam's apple. The Swiss archer William Tell is said to have shot an apple from his son's head. We duck, or bob, for apples at Halloween

parties. Snow White, in the fairy tale, was undone by a poisoned apple.

People say, "An apple a day keeps the doctor away," and it's true that apples are a healthy food. And when we say, "You're the apple of my eye," we mean we are very fond of you, because both you and apples are so appealing. Sweet and tart (often at the same time), crisp, long-lasting, healthful, bright, and colorful, apples are nearly the perfect fruit.

ORANGES

PEOPLE SOMETIMES SAY, "You can't compare apples and oranges." They mean that even two things that look roughly alike (a more or less round fruit, about the size of your fist) are often not the same at all. However, people have been confusing apples and oranges for a very long time now. For instance, the Dutch word for orange, *sinaasappel*, means "China apple." In fact, the "golden apples" mentioned in the previous chapter might well have been oranges. No one really knows.

Oranges first grew in China perhaps 20 million years ago—long before there were people. We know that seeds from one plant may blow in the wind, or roll on the ground, and wind up growing into another plant several inches or even many yards away from the first one. Given enough time, seeds can spread pretty far, if the conditions are right. But once there were people, and once those people figured out that oranges were good to eat, they took the oranges (and their seeds) with them when they traveled, and that's when the spread of oranges really got moving. That's almost certainly how oranges got to the Middle East, to Africa, and then to Europe.

BLOOD ORANGE

When oranges first came to Europe, they were considered a great novelty—so colorful, with such a wonderful smell, and so delicious…and so expensive that only rich people could afford them. In fact, among the fabulously rich, it became the fashion to build elaborate and hugely expensive greenhouses, called orangeries, in which potted orange trees could grow, even though the climate in Europe would not normally allow it.

MANY, MANY YEARS after that, it was Christopher Columbus himself who brought the first orange trees to the New World when he "discovered" America. (Okay, he didn't really discover it, since there were millions of people living here at the time, but that's another story.) 20 years later, an explorer named Ponce de Leon brought oranges to Florida, which today grows roughly 9 billion oranges per year; California grows about 3.75 billion. With so many oranges grown in Florida and California, Americans may be surprised to learn that Brazil is the largest producer of orange juice in the world, followed by the USA in the number two position.

The orange is a citrus fruit. So are the lime, the lemon, the grapefruit, the tangerine (also known as the mandarin orange), the tangelo, the pomelo, the kumquat, and several other more unusual fruits. The differences among them matter a great deal to us—if you bite into a lemon, you'll know right away that it's not an orange. But the odd thing about citrus fruits is that a seed from one can (and often does) grow into a tree that bears almost any of the others. That's why commercial orange growers grow their fruit not from seeds, but from small branches of a tree (called scions),

which are stuck, or grafted, onto the roots of other, older trees (the root stocks). In fact, nearly every orange tree in Florida is grafted onto the roots of a lemon tree.

THE NAVEL ORANGE was named because one end of it looks a bit like your belly button, or navel. It's really a twin— a second, tiny orange tucked inside the first one. The orange is also the only fruit whose name, all by itself, is also a color.

Citrus fruits, including the orange, are very rich in vitamin C (the odds are good that the carton of orange juice in your refrigerator boasts that fact). Without enough vitamin C, people tend to come down with a nasty disease called scurvy, and sailors who were at sea a long time used to get it regularly. That was true until about 200 years ago, when Spain and other European nations began issuing

their sailors lemons to keep them from getting sick. About 50 years later, the British navy began substituting limes for the lemons. To this day, the British are called Limeys.

MARMALADE, a kind of sweet and bitter jam, is usually made with oranges. Oranges—sometimes just the outer skin, called the zest—are also used as a flavoring in many kinds of foods, and also made into a fragrance added to

SOME MEMBERS OF THE CITRUS FAMILY (BUT NOT ALL). *Back row, left to right:* UGLI FRUIT, GRAPEFRUIT, ORANGE. *Front row:* TANGERINE, TANGELO, LIME, LEMON.

cleaning products and deodorizers. But far and away most oranges wind up as juice.

Each year, we Americans drink about 1.5 million gallons of orange juice—that's 4.7 gallons per person. The best of it, of course, is fresh squeezed, but most of it is processed one way or another. A lot of it is frozen concentrate that we thaw and add water to at home. The rest is called fresh, but that doesn't mean it's really fresh squeezed like the ads say. Anyway, it's not clear why we mostly drink it for breakfast. In Brazil they hardly ever drink it at breakfast, but they love it all the rest of the day.

Orange, by the way, is one of the rare instances of a common word that has no rhyme. Really. Try it for yourself. *Silver*, *purple*, and *month* are three more examples.

CORN

FOR US HUMAN BEINGS, surely one of the most important things about any food is its ability to keep us from starving to death. In that sense, corn is by far the most important food in the world. It feeds billions of people, and without it many of them would starve.

The first Europeans ever to see corn were some of Christopher Columbus's men when they landed in Haiti in 1492. The Arawak people who lived there called it *mahiz.* By the time the Europeans got around to spelling it, it came out *maize.* Most of the world still calls it that, although Americans call it *corn,* which in England just means "grain." Whatever you call it, it was clear that corn had been grown in the Americas for a very long time before Columbus showed up.

Actually, corn was developed from a grass called teosinte by Native Americans around 8,000 years before

Columbus even dreamed of sailing here. By spotting and separating teosinte plants that had bigger and better ears, they came up with the plant that now, all these centuries later, feeds the world.

THE COLONISTS who landed in Jamestown, Virginia, in 1607, 115 years after Columbus first sailed to America, probably already knew about corn. Columbus had brought some back with him to Spain, and very soon people were growing it all over Europe. Unfortunately, those colonists didn't think to bring any with them when they sailed to America. Two-thirds of them died that first winter, and it would have been much worse if not for Poca-hontas. She may or may not have saved their leader, Captain John Smith, from the wrath of her father, Powhatan, but she did negotiate to get corn for the starving colonists.

FULL-GROWN TEOSINTE *(left)*
AND MODERN CORN *(right)*

It was pretty much the same story 500 miles north and 13 years later in Plymouth, Massachusetts. A gift of corn from the local Native Americans kept nearly half of the pilgrims alive through their first winter. The following spring, they planted 20 acres of corn, and after the fall harvest, they threw a party for themselves and their Native American friends. History is always more complicated than you think, but we have come to call that party the first Thanksgiving.

TODAY, we use stunning amounts of corn in an amazing number of ways: we feed our farm animals about half of the 10 billion bushels of corn that we grow each year. Those of us lucky enough to have fresh-picked corn eat it right off the cob, but we also eat creamed corn, canned corn, and frozen corn. At the movies (and at home), we eat 1.5 billion pounds of popped corn a year. We grind up the kernels of corn into mush to make polenta and corn pone, or hush puppies, and we grind it up a bit more finely for flour, to make tortillas by the millions and corn bread by the tons.

Of course, nearly everyone at some time or another has had cornflakes—dry breakfast cereals, often with gobs of sugar frosting or other sweeteners on them. They were invented by

KEN ROBBINS

two brothers from Michigan named Kellogg about 100 years ago, and people eat an average of about of 11 pounds of them a year in this country alone. To all that corn add the more than 18 billion pounds of corn syrup that are used every year to sweeten nearly every processed food we eat, and then allow for the 1.8 billion bushels of corn that have recently begun to be used to make ethanol, a new fuel that can be used in place of gasoline.

And then there's the word *corny*. There are lots of ideas about where that came from. Here's one of them that's probably not too far wrong: it wasn't that long ago that 80 percent of American families lived on farms, and a very large portion of those farms, especially in the Midwest, were growing corn. Back then (and perhaps still today), it was the habit of city slickers to look down their noses a bit at country folk, so *corny* came to mean something so simple and unhip that it would only appeal to the country bumpkins who grew corn.

"The corn is as high as an elephant's eye" is a line from a song in the famous musical *Oklahoma*. It's a colorful way of saying that corn is a grass that grows unusually tall—in some varieties, more than eight feet. In fact, the corn grows so tall, and the stalks so close together, that it is not at all impossible to get lost in a field of corn. In some places, corn farmers have even taken to cutting the tall corn into the form of a maze. People come to these farms and pay for the fun of getting lost in the maze of maize.

IN RECENT YEARS, husking corn (pulling off the green outer leaves and removing the silk tassels) has been done by machines, but before there were machines to do it, husking the corn from an entire field was a large, hard, and tiresome job. In the Midwest and elsewhere, friends and neighbors would gather to help out with the task and make a party of it at the same time. It was called a husking bee after the way bees in a hive cooperate to get their bee chores done.

HUMAN BEINGS do seem to like their liquor, and we have learned to make it out of nearly anything that grows—wheat, rye, grapes, berries, potatoes—all widely available in liquor stores. The vast majority of illegal liquor is made from corn. Corn liquor is often called *moonshine* because, being illegal, it's made secretly at night, or else it's called *white lightning*, because it's clear and powerful.

Strangely, people used to like to set the dried leaves of certain plants on fire and then inhale the fumes. Come to think of it, people still do that—it's called smoking. In any case, it used to be common, especially among poor people, to make a cheap pipe out of a piece of corncob.

BANANAS

BANANAS GROW in warm or tropical climates. It seems they were first discovered and grown in the rain forests of Southeast Asia (which certainly are warm and tropical). That was more than 3,000 years ago. Records are a little scarce from this period, but it seems that Arabs (perhaps in the 600s, in the time of Muhammad) brought them back to the Middle East, and from there to Africa.

When the Portuguese landed in Africa, they found bananas growing in large parts of the continent. In different places, the Africans called them *banna*, or *banan*, or even *bnanu*. The Portuguese made it *banana* and promptly took banana plants to the Canary Islands, which (at the time) they owned. (The Canary Islands are off the Atlantic coast of Africa, west of Morocco.)

The Spanish, rivals of the Portuguese, occupied the Canaries and found the bananas there in the 1500s. Not long after that, the Spanish sailed to South America, where they were looking for gold. In the process, they brought disease, misery, and death to the native people there, but they also brought . . . bananas.

PLANTAIN

It turned out, though, that bananas were a very successful crop in South and especially Central America—that's modern-day Honduras, El Salvador, Guatemala, Panama, Costa Rica, and Nicaragua.

Banana republic is a phrase made up by the famous short-story writer O. Henry back in 1904, in a collection of short stories called *Cabbages and Kings*. He was referring to Honduras, but the term came to refer to several of those small countries in Central and South America where many of the poorest people didn't have much choice but to work on large banana plantations. The plantations were owned by big foreign companies—generally from the United States— and the little "republics" were ruled by corrupt dictators and a few of their friends who got rich while most of the people struggled to make a living. Things may have changed for the better since then—but not that much.

EVEN AMONG EXPERTS there is much disagreement about the difference between bananas and plantains, and whether bananas are a kind of plantain, or vice versa.

In any case, what we generally call plantains are more dark red or orange in color, or even green when ripe, and less sweet than bananas, and they are mostly eaten cooked. Bananas, in the familiar bright yellow color, are sweeter and can be eaten raw or cooked, though most of them are eaten raw.

Bananas are one of the few foods in the world that are so full of vitamins, minerals, and nourishment of all kinds that it is possible to eat nothing else and still survive in good health. That's definitely possible . . . but maybe a little boring. Still, for very young children who have no teeth, and for very old people who perhaps have very few left, the soft, moist banana is certainly easy to chew and swallow.

IN THE 1940s, there was a popular Brazilian movie star named Carmen Miranda, who is remembered for her sexy dancing and, mostly, for wearing a huge basket of fruit (often including bananas) on her head. She inspired the United Fruit Company to create a cartoon character named Chiquita Banana for its advertising.

By 1905, bananas had become the only fruit that was available almost everywhere, year-round. India, an admittedly large country, produces 24 billion pounds of bananas a year, but you hardly ever see Indian bananas here—they eat them all.

MAKERS OF BREAKFAST CEREALS urged people to eat them with milk and bananas, and people did just that. The banana split was invented in the first years of the 20th century, when ice cream was still a bit of a novelty. (As usual, there were several different people who claimed to have invented it.) Then there's banana cream pie and banana muffins, banana smoothies, and, of course, people just peel 'em and eat 'em.

Naturally, once you've peeled a banana, you need to dispose of the peel. Most people would put it in the trash, but some inconsiderate types might just throw it on the ground. That's not only unsanitary, but since the moist inner side of the peel is slippery, outright dangerous. At least, that's the notion behind about a million gags in movies and especially cartoons about people slipping on banana peels. It's not likely that it has happened very often, but it does make an irresistible joke.

A BANANA PLANT can grow incredibly fast—as tall as a man in just three months—and reach a height of 20 to 30 feet in a year. It's not a tree, though, it's a bush— admittedly a very tall bush. And it dies every year after producing just one bunch of bananas (that's about a hundred per bunch).

TOMATOES

WE KNOW THAT TOMATOES first grew somewhere in the New World. What we don't know is exactly where in the New World they came from. Some people think it was the west side (the Pacific side) of South America—say, maybe where Peru is now. Others think it was Mexico (south of our border, but really part of North America). Tomatoes, after all, did get their name from the word *tomatl*, which was used by the Aztec people of Mexico.

Hernando Cortés and other Spaniards took the tomato (and much else) from the Aztecs' home to Spain. The warmer areas of Spain and France and especially Italy took to it right away. They used it for salads and cooked it with onions in olive oil to make a tomato sauce pretty much like what we so often use today. (Think of the red stuff you get on spaghetti and pizzas.)

TOMATILLOS

In England, though, and in the American colonies, too, some people thought tomatoes were poison. Although many people ate them and lived, the notion that tomatoes could kill you hung on for quite a while. The story goes that in 1820 a man in Salem, New Jersey, announced that he would eat a basketful of tomatoes right in front of the courthouse. People were supposedly so shocked that anyone would invite a gruesome death in this way that they showed up in the thousands to watch.

STILL, TOMATOES, along with potatoes and eggplants, do belong to the same plant family as the deadly nightshade, a plant that is powerfully poisonous in every part. (Eating just one leaf can kill a grown human.) Tomato leaves and stems really are poisonous, but the tomato itself is safe and even quite healthy (it's a great source of vitamin C). The part that we eat is the fruit of the tomato plant. Contrary to what many believe, tomatoes are fruits and not vegetables, even though they are not sweet.

People had another strange notion about tomatoes, as well. They called them *love apples* and imagined that eating them made people fall in love. That's rubbish, of course, but some people think they know how that idea got started. It seems

BEFORE MOVIES and television, people used to go to theaters to see live performances by singers, dancers, clowns, comedians, and actors. It was called vaudeville, and it was a bit rough and tumble—if the audience didn't like what they saw, they were likely to throw rotten tomatoes at the performers to express their displeasure. That doesn't happen so much anymore, but the phrase *rotten tomatoes* is still used to describe a bad review of any performance.

WE EAT an enormous amount of tomatoes. We grow more of them in our own personal gardens than any other food, and we eat them fresh by the billions in salads and on sandwiches. We eat them as tomato soup, in sauces for spaghetti and on pizza, for barbeque, and, of course, as President Reagan's favorite vegetable: ketchup (sometimes spelled *catsup*).

that the Italians thought the tomato came from the Moors of Africa, so they called it (reasonably enough, but falsely) *pomo di Moro*, which translates as "apple of the Moors." (It helps if you know that the Moors were Muslims from Africa who, after a bit of fighting, settled for quite awhile in southern Spain and brought with them many new things, including the secrets of papermaking and a vast knowledge of science, medicine, and architecture.) To make matters worse, *pomo di Moro* sounded a lot like *pomo d'amore*, which in Italian means "apple of love." History, it seems, is sometimes as much about misunderstandings as anything else.

Ketchup, by the way, has been around for quite some time. Long before they even knew about tomatoes, the Chinese had a sauce they called *kat siap*, which was made from the brine of pickled fish. The idea, and the name, spread around the world, and the main ingredient was sometimes walnuts, mushrooms, cranberries, even anchovies, or any number of other things. The first-known recipes for tomato ketchup are a little over 200 years old. Americans still use an enormous amount of ketchup, but largely because there are now more Hispanic people in the United States than there were earlier, salsa (a sauce made with raw tomatoes, lime juice, chili peppers, onions, and cilantro leaves) has surpassed ketchup in popularity.

MOST PEOPLE think of tomatoes as round and smooth and, when ripe, evenly red orange in color, but it wasn't always so. All too often, the best-tasting food is not necessarily the best looking, or the most convenient for the people who sell them. These days, we are beginning to see more of what are called heirloom tomatoes. They come from old seeds, handed down from one generation to the next, and they produce tomatoes that taste better than they look, as opposed to most commercially grown tomatoes, which look a lot better than they taste.

RIPENING HEIRLOOM TOMATO

POTATOES

L IKE CORN, potatoes are a really important source of nutrition in the world. Also like corn, the potato began in what was later called South America (in Peru, to be more specific), and it was grown and developed by Native Americans (for nearly 8,000 years) before Europeans (the Spanish explorers) brought it back to Europe. That was about 50 years after Columbus had first brought back corn. Potatoes didn't catch on quite as quickly as corn did, but once they did, they were being grown and eaten nearly everywhere.

Potatoes are tubers—fleshy parts of the potato plant that grow underground, like the roots. Potato plants do produce flowers, but the flowers often don't produce any seeds. In any case, new potato plants can and do grow from the "eyes" of old potatoes. (If you've ever left some potatoes around the house too long, you've probably seen them sprout.) Farmers grow their potato crops from seed potatoes—which are not seeds at all, but little pieces of cut-up potatoes, each of which includes at least one "eye." The farmer plants these pieces in the ground—as if they were seeds—and within weeks little potato plants arise.

A FRESHLY BAKED POTATO is very hot, and it can only be held in the hand for a brief moment before you get burned. From that fact came the idea of a children's game where players stand in a circle and toss a ball or a beanbag among themselves as rapidly as possible—as if it were a hot potato.

Potatoes took longer to be widely grown in Europe than corn, but once they were, many countries came to really depend on them for food. Especially in Ireland, but elsewhere as well, poor people were forced to rely almost exclusively on potatoes. It wasn't ideal, but it kept most of them alive until, in 1845 and then again in 1846, almost the entire potato crop was wiped out by a disease called potato blight. No one really knows for sure how many people died of starvation, but it could certainly be counted in the hundreds of thousands, if not millions.

Potatoes are sometimes called *spuds* because of the spadelike tool (a small shovel, really) called a spud used to dig them out of the earth. In other languages, they are called *erdappfels* (Bavarian), *aardapples* (Dutch), and *pommes de terre* (French)— all three names mean "earth-apple" or "fruit of the earth."

COUCH POTATOES are lazy people who mostly lie around on a couch (as likely as not eating potato chips while watching TV)—kind of the way a potato just lies around in the ground.

In England, thin, crisp, fried slices of potato are called (logically enough) *crisps*, while we call them *potato chips*. Also, what we call French fries the British call *chips*. And, finally, French people don't call French fries *French fries* at all; they call them *pommes frites*, which translates literally as "fried apples," but really means "fried potatoes." Got all that?

Unlike most raw vegetables, raw potatoes don't taste very good, and most people would never eat them that way. We do like them baked, roasted, boiled, and perhaps most of all, fried. We use them in stews and soups, in potato pancakes (sometimes called *latkes*), hash browns, home fries, potato salad, dumplings, knishes, and, of course, just mashed.

FIELD OF POTATO PLANTS

POMEGRANATES

POMEGRANATES were first grown in Iran (once known as Persia), and they spread to other areas with warm, dry climates, including parts of Africa and India. Many are also now grown in the southern part of California, but they are still associated with the Middle East, where they are much more commonly used in food recipes than anywhere else in the world. The fruit, about the size of an adult's fist, grows on a shrub or small tree.

Long ago, the word *apple* was used a little carelessly for any number of fruits (as you may have noticed), so it may not be that surprising that the name *pomegranate* means "apple with many seeds." If you cut one open, it's easy to see why—the inside is filled with hundreds and hundreds of juicy red seeds like perfect gleaming rubies (or, if you prefer, like glistening drops of fresh . . . blood!).

The pomegranate has an important place in Greek mythology. Demeter was the Greek goddess of the harvest. But when her daughter, Persephone, was carried off by Hades, the dark lord of the underworld, she wept and moaned and cursed,

and in general was too upset to make all the green things of the world grow. That meant no food for the earth, so Zeus, the king of the gods, commanded Hades to release Persephone, and Hades had no choice but to obey. Still, there was a catch—a rule of the Fates, whom even Zeus could not ignore. The rule was that mortals could never return from the underworld if they ate anything there—anything at all! Persephone knew the rule and desperately wished to go home, so she went without food. Hades, however, tricked her into eating just four pomegranate seeds before she left. That meant that though she could go home, for eternity she has to return to the under-world every year for four months. For those months of winter, Demeter weeps again and nothing grows.

THOUGH APPLES AND ORANGES and even bananas are sometimes mentioned as the fateful fruit eaten by Adam and Eve in the story of the Garden of Eden, scholars point out that none of those fruits was known to have grown in the Middle East in ancient times. The pomegranate, however, just might have been the one.

HAND GRENADE

Two explosive devices—the grenade and its smaller brother, the hand grenade—get their names from the pomegranate. This is partly because of their shapes, which are similar, and partly because the outsides of the weapons are divided up into small pieces (all the better to kill and maim), and those small pieces reminded people of the many grains, or seeds, inside the pomegranate. Less horribly, the garnet, a red gemstone, also gets its name from the same fruit.

A SWEET SYRUP made from pomegranate juice is called *grenadine*. The chances are that if you were ever served a "child's cocktail" like a Roy Rogers or a Shirley Temple, it was sweetened and made a rosy red color with a splash of grenadine. Pomegranate juice is also used to dye fabrics and is sometimes put on a cut to kill germs.

GRAPES

WE EAT WHOLE GRAPES as a snack. We certainly eat grape jelly and drink grape juice. The Greeks have a dish called *dolmades*— herbs and rice and often meat wrapped in grape leaves. Dried grapes, or raisins, go in our cereal, among other things, and grape flavor is used in everything from soda to chewing gum.

The vast majority of the grapes we grow are for making wine. The grapes are picked (at just the right time), gathered, and crushed. Then the juice is put in a huge vat and allowed to ferment. Fermenting happens naturally when tiny, one-celled fungi called yeast cause some of the sugar in the grape juice to turn into alcohol. At that point, the grape juice has become wine, and if you are a child, you are generally not allowed to drink it until you're older. The reason for this is simple: a little bit of alcohol, when it is drunk, makes people feel good, but just a very small amount more also robs them of their ability to think clearly. Adults, who may legally drink, tend to believe that children don't think all that clearly in the first place and should, therefore, never drink. It should be noted that some of those adults who drink probably shouldn't either.

IT'S NOT EXACTLY CERTAIN when humans first made wild grapes into wine. It definitely would have been almost impossible before the invention of pottery around 9,000 years ago—after all, what would they have kept it in? Anyway, wine making might have begun as early as 8,000 years ago. Guesses about where this may have happened include Georgia (not the state in the American South, but the country, once part of the Soviet Union), Iraq, and Iran.

Wine is mentioned many times in the Bible. It is sometimes described there as a wonderful thing and sometimes as a great evil. The same could certainly be said today.

WINE MAKING is depicted on the walls of ancient Egyptian tombs, and scientists can tell that five clay storage bottles buried with the pharaoh known as King Tut (Tutankhamun)

contained white wine. Wine was loved and made by the ancient Greeks, who had a special god of wine called Dionysos. The ancient Romans called their wine god Bacchus.

Nearly 500 years before Columbus landed in the Caribbean, Leif Ericson sailed from Norway and found grapes in Nova Scotia. In fact, he called the land Vinland ("vine land") because there were so many wild grape vines growing there. Of course, there are many kinds of grapes, and the ones growing back then in America weren't particularly good for making wine. Many years later, Thomas Jefferson, the third American president, tried to grow the European kind of grape vines in Virginia, but he had no luck. The climate in California is much better for these kinds of grapes, and today there is a whole lot of wine being made there (approximately half a billion gallons a year).

TODAY, wine still has strong connections with religion. In Judaism, it is drunk on holy days, and in the Catholic Church, it is used in the celebration of Mass. Wine was so important to Spanish Catholics in the 1500s that when they went to South America, they brought grape vines with them so that they could make wine for their religious ceremonies. Wine, and all alcohol, is forbidden in the Islamic faith.

MUSHROOMS

MUSHROOMS are not really plants, exactly—they're fungi (the plural of fungus). Like plants, they don't move about the way animals generally do, and they do have a primitive kind of seed called spores. But unlike plants, they don't get their energy from the sun. Instead, they get the nutrients they need exclusively from the ground or from the plants (often trees) on which they grow.

Some of them, if you eat them, will affect your body in ways that can make you very sick or even kill you. That is a bit weird, and you can see where some people might be put off. Three varieties of amanita mushroom are poisonous to human beings. One is called *Amanita phalloides*, also known as the Death Cup; another is *Amanita verna*, also called the Angel of Death. The third is *Amanita muscaria*, or Fly Agaric. Eating any one of them can be lethal.

For a number of reasons, mushrooms have a reputation as magical. Eating certain mushrooms can affect your mind in odd ways, causing visions, trances, and very strange feelings, indeed. Some Native American tribes and certain groups in Siberia use these mushrooms as part of their religious ceremonies. In *Alice's Adventures in Wonderland* by Lewis Carroll, a caterpillar sits on a mushroom and tells Alice that if she eats one side of the mushroom it will make her larger, and the other side will make her smaller. In the book, anyway, it works.

Anyone who lives outside of a city has seen mushrooms—sometimes pretty good-sized ones—just pop up within hours of rain. In fact, anything that grows really fast—a fashion, say, or a new housing development—is said to "mushroom." Some mushrooms grow so fast it does seem magical. But it's not. Like everything in nature, it's quite . . . natural.

MOREL

A MUSHROOM is really just the parts of the fungus that you see, which are the cap and the stem. Beneath that, in the ground on which the mushroom grows, there is the mycelium, a network of thin fibers that you could think of as the root of the mushroom. While the mushroom itself might seem to spring up overnight, the mycelium may have been growing underground for months or even years.

AMANITA MUSCARIA

The fibers of the mycelium are extremely thin, but sometimes they can spread out over a VERY large area. There is a fungus of this sort called *Armillaria gallica* in Crystal Falls, Michigan, which scientists think may be spread out (underground) over 37 acres and weigh nearly 100 tons. That would make it the largest single living thing in the world. People in Crystal Falls, and some others, as well, with tongue in cheek, call it the humungous fungus. It's also guessed that it might be more than 2,400 years old.

THE WORD *toadstool* is used for mushrooms that are inedible or poisonous. Why? Well, mushrooms with a cap and stalk do look more than a bit like stools, sized just about right for most toads, I'd guess, and some toads can themselves be very poisonous.

The phrase *fairy ring* refers to a circular arrangement of mushrooms that can be seen fairly often in the woods or in fields when conditions are right. Fanciful people coming upon these rings may have imagined that the rings resulted from fairies doing a circle dance.

Mushrooms, as a species, are very old, and they exist in most parts of the world, especially where there is plenty of rainfall. Throughout history, people gathered wild mushrooms rather than growing them. (Knowledge of mushroom growing was rare until the 1700s.) To recognize the good ones and avoid the bad ones took (and still takes) great skill

THE VAST MAJORITY of the mushrooms we eat are the common white field mushroom. They're grown in cool, dark places (often in caves), harvested, and sold in supermarkets. Mushroom growers also produce the big portobello mushroom, Japanese shitake and enoki mushrooms, chanterelles, porcini, and many more varieties in great numbers. Other mushrooms, like morels, still can't be grown and must be found by mushroom hunters.

We eat mushroom soup and have them for toppings on steaks and burgers and pizzas, in stews and risottos. In French cooking, there is a mushroom paste (with shallots and herbs and butter) called duxelles, and it is used in all kinds of soups and stuffings and sauces. Strangely enough, wild mushrooms are also an excellent source of colorful dyes for fabrics.

and knowledge. People who study mushrooms are called mycologists; people who hunt them in the woods and fields are called . . . mushroomers. Mistakes often cost people a bout of terrible illness if not their very lives. Still, poor people often needed mushrooms to have enough to eat, and rich people were happy to pay for the ones that were rare and delicious.

Though they are not exactly mushrooms, truffles are another kind of fungus that grows underground. They are rare and very expensive and must be found using special truffle hounds or truffle pigs, who can locate them by smell. The best truffles are found only in Europe—black ones in France, white ones in Italy.

FOOD FOR THOUGHT

EVERY HUMAN BEING, including you and me, must eat or die; as of 2007, there were more than 6.5 billion of us in the world. What we eat and how much depends on who we are, where we are, and how fortunate or unfortunate we happen to be. Our supply of foods is also profoundly affected by storms, droughts, wars, and diseases all over the globe. By 2050, the population of the world perhaps will have doubled, and growing or finding enough food for everyone is going to be quite a challenge. Just a few generations ago, the vast majority of Americans lived or worked on a farm. Now it's just 2 percent of us who do. As a result, most of us know less and less about where our food comes from; in many cases, we don't even really know what it looks like in its natural state.

Every food does have a story, and every one I've looked into so far has been fascinating. My hope is that readers of this book will take the time to look into the history of at least one of their favorite foods—or one of their least favorite foods—or maybe even a kind of food they never even thought much about before. That would be food for thought.

— KEN ROBBINS